ISBN: 0692102345
ISBN-13: 978-0-692-10234-3

Design & Illustration: Lauren Hurst
pg. 11, 19, 26, 29, 32, 39, 42, 48, 54, 60, 65, 73, 81, 87

from sky to sea

shelby leinbach

dedications

to my husband, Anthony, for his faith, patience, and support, and for loving me just as i am.

to my parents, for their example of love for Jesus.

to my Savior, for reaching down into the sea and saving me.

about the book

everything i've ever wanted to write, think, and feel up to this point in my life has gone into the very binding of this book. the amount of love and hope radiating from its very existence is to bring you the joy i've found in being swept up from the depths of the ocean i once was in. even i need my own words. even i need to soak in every one of them daily, only because they've been given to me by my loving Creator – to instill in me a passionate purpose. you reading these words right now mean that all of heaven is working on behalf of your prayers for hope and healing. Someone bigger than life itself allowed you to hold this book in your hands right now; that in itself is nothing short of a miracle.

this book is a collection of my writings and poems thus far in my life, and it symbolizes the verse i mentioned in psalm about being pulled from ocean-depths to the skies of new life. all words in this book are not capitalized except for the words referring to God because to me, that symbolizes the significance He brings into life; i want Him to be capital in my writings rather than what i have to say. i love visual representations, so i hope you gain the same perspective from that as i did.

too often, we carry weights within us – this book is a hope to be carried. it's meant to be simple and straightforward, introspective, and minimal yet impactful. it holds my overflow of peace and words to bring rest to your mind, as they did to mine. thank you for answering the call on your life to absorb the positivity that only He can bring. my wish is that you take these words and pass them on – because every person on earth needs to know how loved they are by their Maker and how much worth they hold.

and go in love,
and make peace a part of your very being.

you were, are, and always will be enough.

all my love (and His),
—*s. l.*

but me He caught — reached all the way
from sky to sea; He pulled me out
of that ocean of hate, that enemy chaos,
the void in which i was drowning.

—psalm 18:16–19 (msg)

humble

the King of my heart
came as a King
only at heart

the Author

all He wants
is your heart
your time
your unspoken thoughts
the feelings beneath your skin
because
He wrote the deepest parts
of who you are
and to Him,
you are no mystery

soul

a body is a body,
skin, merely skin,
but
a soul
is heaven's gold

wings

the world may leave you
with clipped wings,
but your heart can fly
and will soar
to higher highs

colors

if His promises
formed the rainbow
then His promises
will bring color
where my life
is left
black and white

servant

our King became less
so we could become more

proverbs 31

but,
it doesn't mention
what she looks like
the color of her hair,
or that she is the most
beautiful
no – it's her character,
her strength,
her nobility
that defines her
true worth

november 19

and He always reveals Himself
in bits and pieces of light
so we are never without hope;
you'll find your light

His

we are heaven's missing pieces
and He just wants us back

do you feel that pulse?
it's the life inside your veins
everything you are is
living
breathing
wanting
for a greater purpose.
don't compromise anything else
for this privilege
yes — it's an honor to even be alive
here on this earth.
go and seek your mission,
put fear and anxiety on eviction notice in your mind.
because a life filled with true
purpose
and
worth
cannot be stopped

—*your purpose*

truths

you're a carrier of miracles
you hold eternity in your heart
(you have so much to offer)

recovery

He collected my tears
one
by
one
and watered my soul
and made gardens
in the places where
the demons stole

10 o'clock thoughts

tomorrow may hold everything,
or nothing,
and that's okay
He's holding your hand whispering,
"I'm in every one of your days."

your end
His beginning

—hope

her

and her beauty
doesn't come from the colors in her eyes,
but the way her words
paint colors and pictures in her book
over her favorite cup of tea;
her beauty
doesn't come from the glow on her skin from the sun
but from the way she glows when
she tells of her deepest passions
and the people she loves
and her Savior
not from the brands in her closet,
not from the numbers on her tags,
or the numbers on the scale
not from the things
vying for her behind glass windows,
or what she thinks she needs
but from her soul,
from her inner being,
that don't ever need
brands
products
surgery
trends
editing –
because it takes
different eyes
and
different mind
to really see
her

reality

and we cannot believe the lies
coming from the flawed and broken,
when we are surrounded by the truth
of the One who is perfect

matthew 11:28

just as we feel our bodies rise
and feel lighter than air
when we let something heavy down,
so it is with our souls — our spirits rise when we lay our
burdens down to Him

reasons why we feel

the reason we were molded and fashioned
to feel so strongly,
love so deeply,
want so endlessly,
is because of the eternity in our hearts
and the way it's supposed to be
with Him
but
we end up feeling everything too strongly,
loving the wrong things too deeply,
wanting the wrong things endlessly
but when we point our inner enigmas
and raging storms within us to the One who
comprehends them
and makes the chaos calm
He restores our
feelings
wants
and love
back
to Him

daisy

you haven't fallen back,
or felt the depths of a certain feeling for no reason at all
no — you've broken ground.
solid, concrete ground.
you had to break it with every ounce of feeling within you.
and now, you're here for all the world to marvel at.

nightfall

the sun set
and my feelings rose
I needed You the most

reflecting

i once held (firmly) the pen that
vigorously scribbled the text
in the book of my life
wondering
why
it all made no sense.
but once i gave up the pen
and handed it to You
You translated it
into Your thoughts
and Your words
finally
making sense of it all

how high, how deep

high mountain peaks
deeper seas
and yet,
His love
exceeds

epiphany

every little piece of you is the whole, beautiful idea of a Great
Maker. He thought you would be a brilliant idea for His earth.
He surrounded you with beauty, wrote a transcript for your life,
and set you into motion.
He watches and waits for you to find Him.
He hopes and prays you have open eyes to see Him,
open ears to hear Him,
and open hands to praise Him.
He feels the weight of deception you feel.
He feels the sting of confusion you carry.
but even still, He remains the Greatest Spirit,
the Greatest Force.
He reaches into time and space and wipes our slates clean, with
every bought of pain and sorrow.
no other being can do this for you. no other being loves you with
His love.
the stars connect the heavens together,
and the depths of the sea hold the foundations of the earth,
but none can be greater than the Maker of them all.
and He is the Maker of you.

meaning

the very fact that your eyes are
scanning these pages
and your lungs are
taking in air
points to the absolute meaning
your life has
(and Life itself is glad you are here)

will your storms yield
flowers
or
ruin?

—*i hope they yield endless gardens*

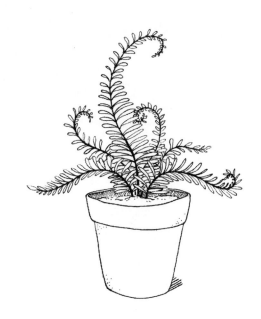

found

You found me
when i lost myself

the ears of the world are ever
hearing, hearing, hearing,
but all of heaven is listening
to the very language of your soul

—*you are infinitely heard*

façade

our minds will spend too much time
trying to convince us that
we are never enough
to be afraid
to never take that risk
i'd hate to live my life that way
under the counterfeit reality that my mind
stopped me from so much
and that it was all just a façade

peace

i found Peace like an old friend
waiting, behind an old book
it looked like it had been waiting there
for some time
but it didn't waste any time
rushing out of its chair, throwing down the dusty
old book
to meet me there
saying "i knew you'd come back,
"i knew you'd find me again."
it met me like a river meets the sea,
it soaked through my desert soul
it unpacked its bags in the home of my heart.
Peace never left,
it waited
waited
waited
until I remembered His name
and remembered my own
and who I am
and who I am without Him.

consider

but
did you
remember
to dress
your heart
in its
sunday
best
too?

to be known

my soul has a voice
that only He can hear
a language, only He can translate
i am known,
and knowing that
completes me

appearances

many see the beauty of a flower
in its petals;
few see its beauty
in the way it grew

what if

what if
He calmed the storm-ridden seas
to show He can quiet the gale-force winds
inside of me, too
what if
He healed those
who were untouchable
to show He can heal the deepest parts of me
that are untouchable, too
what if
I'm alive right now,
breathing out these words
because He gave Himself up to death
so these words
could exist
i'm learning that
for every 'what if',
He did

i passed a man while driving
homeless;
with his bags by his side
his disheveled appearance
my heart was pained, i couldn't bear
to look him in the eye

one thing i saw
the cardboard sign in his hands,
holding the words
that made my heart sink
below my chest
and made me understand

"i need a miracle" it read
why did i pass by?
when i carry the very Miracle
he needs inside?

> so then i knew; he's not the only one
> he's a picture of the whole earth
> of every soul, every being
> needing the One

> He's the Miracle we all desperately need
> and He told me that day:

> "I sent you that man
> so you could see how much
> the world needs you here
> and needs your words,
> and that you are grafted into My Plan.

> because of him, these words are here
> on this page,
> and for your soul to hear

temporary

but every hue, all the colors of my hair,
they will fade
my skin will form cracks and wrinkles,
the tempo of my heart
will slow
all of me will fade from the earth,
my temporary home,
this temple of mine
but my soul will be freed,
its the essence of heaven;
the spirit of me is forever

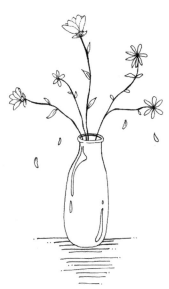

7:45am

i woke up later
than i'd hoped
my heart
a little distant
thoughts
trailing, wandering, aimless
somehow,
though i'm wicked
in the name of being complacent
i'm ok;
i'm moving forward
and shown mercy
either way

simple love

His love is immense (immeasurable)
yet, so simple

it feels like a warm, inviting café
with a soft acoustic track playing
the smell of something baking
and ground coffee
nothing fancy

it feels like the way eyes look
when someone's smiling
and the glow of the evening through sheer curtains

it feels like home
when you're somewhere off the map

it feels like everything good
and honest
and that will always be
the most beautiful thing to me

who

if you woke up one day
and the mirror
showed no reflection,
if your external
left you
and the world only saw
your soul
who would
you be?

strength

but
even if you fall
you have the chance
to prove your strength

you are needed

your table, your reserved seat,
is there, quietly waiting for you
to take your weight, to let you set your bags down
and stay awhile (forever)
your table is sure; never moving or changing
and there,
peace is the air you breathe
mercy, the ground you walk upon
and He is seated
on the other side
with love written in His eyes
looking at you
like
you're
the
greatest
human
alive
and He says "come,"
"I've needed you here."

awe–struck

we go to the mountain top,
catch the milky way decorating
the jet-black sky,
and feel it move our inner being

we watch the ocean waves
touch the sky
and come crashing down
filling our minds with peace
with the sound it brings

the formations of rocks,
the flower-freckled fields,
the songs of the earth colliding
enigmatic to our eyes,
deeper than our skin

not that the stars are our gods,
nor the seas, our commander
the mountains may move us,
but they bow at His name

His spirit
was left in this planet
when He breathed everything to life
and it all connects our souls back
to His

paradox

be delicate enough to feel

become strong enough to understand

deeper than skin

what a God we have
who wants nothing more than
to be felt and loved with our souls
than to be seen

i am becoming

i lived a day
i will never live again
i was given those
twenty-four hours
to do something with
to shed another layer
of pride
guilt
shame
insecurity
selfishness
greed
to water my seeds of
love
selflessness
humility
patience
gratitude
if i live another day
without this crucial
coming to oneself
of what i must do
with every single day
i will have never lived
wholly nor fully
without possibly ever
becoming me

awareness

little by little
learning
each day given to me
studying
the intricacies of moments
i'll never feel again
letting my mind
comprehend the things
i can only gain
here and now

my favorite place

i believe
in the way the salty air dances
around my sun-kissed skin
and through my messy hair
i believe
in the way the ocean sings
a song of peace to me
a sound
only my soul can take in
i believe
in these heaven-sent moments
they bring me somewhere
only i can go
for me, only
He makes
the edge of the world
feel
like
home

seashell

you've been through
those perilous waves
yet
here you are — so beautiful
and brave

heaven's
more than a place;

you are His heaven

—*who you are to Him*

true love

Love did not come
to build His throne
Love came
to leave it

depth

giving in is easy,
to wade in shallow waters
is safe
but deeper still,
underneath the surface
a certain depth is found;
so take your ship out,
dive down and find
the things that live there
whether good
or bad
and let them change you
shape you
make you
teach you
to feel depth
to experience life
to become you

perspective

whoever sees you
as someone unworthy,
unlovable,
unwanted,
it's not that you are
those things;
they themselves
need to know that
they aren't unworthy
unlovable
and unwanted
(you should let them know that)

the choice

you could choose to avoid it
or
you could choose to defeat it

eclipse

if He who set alignment
to the planets
and brought the stars to life

how
much
more

does He have your life
set into alignment
with divine purpose

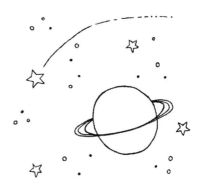

the ocean at 8pm

i stood at the edge of the waves,
and thought of you.

you are a vast sea of beauty,
often tossed violently by winds and tides,
but at day's end,
when the sun disappears beyond the dunes
and heaven's colors fill the atmosphere,
you're at peace;
a piece of heaven on earth.

indefinitely loved

even though
you could never truly
earn love
it always ends up
finding its way into your life

He is an ocean

shades of ocean
painted for me
with heaven's colors
it's hard to believe
of all the wonders
of all the things
in all the world
my eyes can see
the closest i feel to my Maker
is at the sea

pursuit

You have my heart
yet
You move heaven
and earth
to chase after me

seeds of hope

in time, we will all reach the point where certain evils lose
their grip on us, and peace becomes our crown.
our smiles, more genuine,
our countenance glowing,
the darkest corners finally filled with light.
all of the unspoken prayers,
the tear-soaked thoughts,
the seeds from those things will eventually bloom like
wildflowers in your soul.
you are alive for that.
you are here to experience His peace.

state of mind

that morning,
i woke up with the sea
and listened as the waves
whispered His thoughts to me
He said, "My peace is an ocean,
where heaven and earth collide
a place of comfort
you carry inside;
so take your ocean-mind
it's always filled with Me,
it will never run out –
a sea that never runs dry."

temple

i once was abandoned,
felt the void inside my veins
i was neither something
or nothing
just empty space
but light streamed through my cracks
and warmed my coldest parts
i became His temple
His spirit, His home
in the caverns of my heart
i was meant
to be filled
with something other than myself

Ocean-Calmer

the winds lost their course
and the sea rose high,
but just one word
and the dust settled,
the waters fell quiet,
and so did the winds
and restless seas
inside my soul

august morning

there is so much
good
waiting for you today
will you let it in?
will you let it cover you
like sunlight on your skin?
like your favorite song?
let it,
because it will begin
to shape you
into you

affirmation

don't you see?
no one else has your mind,
your spirit is your own,
your words are a treasure

don't ever hold back your thoughts
your words
what you have to offer

because the world needs it
and the world needs you

He is love

i learned that
i never needed love
to save me –
love Himself
came to rescue me

reminders –

– if you could see your soul,
it is far more beautiful than anything ever seen.

– you were bought with a price that is immeasurable.

– you are covered in infinite love.

sky

we would find it odd
if a bird
never once left her nest,
and never used
her wings
we would question why
a butterfly
became a new creature
from that encasement,
but never flew away
i wonder why
your soul has beautiful wings
yet its so comfortable
living in a cage;
your soul is a caged bird
a flightless butterfly,
and though you were born of earth,
you were destined for
the sky

10,000 times

we all reach a moment where
we come up out of the water,
gasping and filling our lungs with crystal-clear air
all because of a hand that decided
to reach down,
see us as reachable
rather than lost to the depths,
who came from the safety
and prominence of heights
to take us up to a new view,
with new eyes
who didn't have to,
but did.

i now walk with Him on the shore
with the waters in my sights,
and although i often go out
a little too far
again and again,
for every time i do
He would do it
10,000 times.

we need you

i think it's lovely –
when you are
who you are
shamelessly
(be that more)

fighter

fool your demons.
remind them that they have zero power
over the spirit inside of you.
they don't have the privilege of your precious energy.
put the fear right back into them that they put into you.
the more you trick them, the harder it will become for them to
influence you.

your soul is worth fighting for.

faded rose

and there i found
on the faded rose in my jar
she is alive.
she is growing.

in the face of death,
live.

gratitude

while the world listens to the voices
telling them to have more,
i'm learning to pay more attention
to the whisper saying i actually thrive on less

unseen

but promise me
you won't miss the way the horizon is painted
the softest gold and blue
for you

promise me
you won't close your eyes
to the things that are lovely
and unaltered
in a counterfeit world

don't miss
the untouched
the unspoken
the unseen;

what is felt with our spirit's eyes
is what helps us
actually see

sunrise

my soul's rising
is the sunrise
He loves to watch

He takes pride
in the humbling of me
He is kind
towards the darkness in me

to watch a sunrise, it takes patience
to watch my soul rise, He has enough patience

ocean moments

the air dropped down
five degrees
the sand and salty air
mingled with the sea
i took a breath in, filled my lungs
and let myself become
one
with this feeling, unmatched
the ocean aura
the pastel skies of the coast;
these
moments
i
crave
the
most

i know He's God,
but He made me like Him, too
so the way i feel
when i'm loved
believed in
hoped for
and told that i'm enough,
He finds my same joy
when i make Him believe those things, too

—do you believe in Him
the way He believes in you?

too many of us
are huddled in the afternoon sun-lit corners
of our favorite cafés
feeling like a space
that is insignificant –
too many of us
feel like we stick out
rather than stand out
but
too many of us
fail to believe
that we add to this world
yet we subtract ourselves from the equation
and find our hiding places;
too many of us
are slowly
but surely
learning to bring our souls
out of hiding

*(you are not a waste of space. you exist because you are
needed.)*

wholeness

if you live your life based on the truth
that you as a whole are already enough,
every part of your life will start to become whole.

the One who is enough,
only created that which is enough.

seen

we live in a world
so desperately wanting to be seen
embedded into our core
the need to be recognized

but we are already loved
and fully known
by the One
who already loves
and sees us

october

the bravest thing
is to give up our parts
while He is making us look beautiful
in the changing

there is so much of you
you haven't seen yet
like the faces
and the mountains
and the oceans
and places
where a different sun sets
He's bringing you through
the exploration of you –
and there is so much incredible you
that the world will get

as in heaven

don't be the one waiting for heaven to appear –
appear as though heaven is already here

good morning

if this morning your eyes found the morning light,
bringing your entire being back into the wondrous life
you've been given, it's for a purpose.
a reason that's all yours to find out.
don't settle for less than finding out why you were so
mercifully woken up again today.

if He holds the universe
He is holding your world together

what i needed

i asked Him to help me grow
and a storm came;
never before had i felt such rain
but it wasn't long before my roots sank deep
infused with grace
unexpected, yet intended
to move me from that place

now i've grown because of the rain –
now i understand why the storm came

my mind is not the place
for a vortex of worry

it was made for the higher things

it was made for the presence of heaven

release what you thought you needed to keep
locked inside of your heart to Him.
open your hands –
be willing to shed your realities and offer them up to the
only One who can create the reality you were created to
live in.

you are so much more than a counterfeit world.

—*a prayer for yourself*

even my own body
never looks at its wounds as something
permanent
it chooses healing
every time

and my soul's healing
cannot be an option

my soul needs my choosing
of healing *every time*

it's okay

the sea rises high
the earth sometimes quakes –
and we will all do the same
and it's okay
because it won't always be that way

mustard seed

give Him a corner of your soul
and He will fill the rooms of your heart with peace
speak a silent prayer
with tear–stained cheeks
and His spirit will scream the voices away
open up your empty hands
and He will place His presence there
close your eyes and plant the smallest seed
and He will make gardens grow
everything we offer
we come up short from
He meets
oh it's enough
it's always more than enough

the top of your mountain is your own place,
a safe space;
you climbed so far to get there

the top of your mountain is not to be compared
to anyone else's;
it's where you rise

and you will get to look down at everything that tried to
stop you

realization

even if life somehow took my breath away,
i would still exhale His truth.

even if only a few eyes fall upon my words,
He still gains the glory.

even if you aren't recognized by the whole world,
you are known by the One who created it.

better

i thought
i could pull my hair back
slip a sweater on
turn my face towards the sun's rising
breathe my billionth breath and
do a little better;
my mind always catches the train that thinks that way
but
in between my thoughts
and disheveled ways
He smiled and it painted today with grace

and though my body
keeps going
and my heart
refuses to stop beating
i will keep continuing
even when my mind
wants to stop
and freeze time

and i will keep continuing

because everything within me
was created to